RAND McNALLY

DISCOVERY ATLAS OF ANIMALS

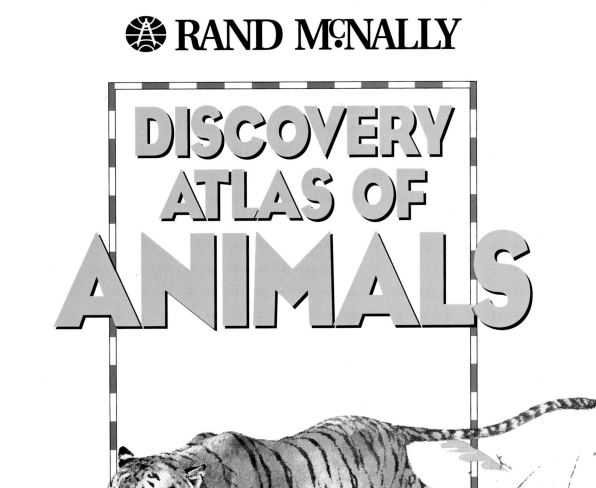

Rand McNally for Kids™

Books•Maps•Atlases

Discovery Atlas of Animals

General manager: Russell L. Voisin
Executive editor: Jon M. Leverenz
Editor: Elizabeth Fagan Adelman
Production editor: Laura C. Schmidt
Manufacturing planner: Marianne Abraham

Rand McNally Discovery Atlas of Animals
Copyright © 1993 by Rand McNally & Company
Published and printed in the United States of America

Portions of this book were originally published in Rand McNally's *Children's Atlas of World Wildlife*, copyright ©1993, 1990 by Rand McNally. Every effort has been made to trace the copyright holders of the photographs in this publication. Rand McNally apologizes in advance for any unintentional omissions and would be pleased to insert the appropriate acknowledgment in any subsequent edition of this book.

Library of Congress Cataloging-in-Publication Data

Rand McNally and Company.
    Discovery atlas of animals.
        p.   cm.
    At head of title: Rand McNally.
    Includes index.
    ISBN 0-528-83579-3
    1. Zoogeography--Maps for children.   I. Title.   II. Title:
Rand McNally discovery atlas of animals.
G1046.D4R3   1993 <G&M>
591.9'022'3--dc20
                                                    93-7252
                                                      CIP
                                                    MAP AC

Contents

Europe

The great northern forests of Europe begin in Norway and extend into Sweden, Finland, and Russia. To the south of these forests is another belt of woodlands. It runs eastward between northern Spain and the United Kingdom, and all across central Europe. Mountainous, or alpine, Europe consists largely of the Alps. The Alps are made up of many mountain ranges in central and southern Europe.

Woodland

To the south of the northern polar regions lies a thick belt of forests. These forests are largely made up of evergreens—pine, spruce, and fir trees. South of these forests are more forests, this time made up of trees such as oak, birch, and maple. These trees shed their leaves each fall.

Alpine

The Alps of Europe are mountains with many scenic peaks. Beginning in southeastern France, these mountains run eastward across Switzerland, northern Italy, southern Germany, and Austria, and into Slovakia. Other mountains of Europe include the Pyrenees, which form the border between France and Spain. The Carpathian Mountains of eastern Europe form another group of major European mountains.

ICELAND

Arctic Circle

FAEROE ISLANDS

Atlantic Ocean

IRELAND

Edinburgh

UNITED KINGDOM

Manchester

London

Brussels

Paris

FRANCE

Rhône River

PYRENEES

ANDORRA

PORTUGAL

SPAIN

Madrid

Barcelona

Lisbon

BALEARIC ISLANDS

GIBRALTAR

Medi

0°

Norwegian Sea

Barents Sea

URAL MOUNTAINS

SWEDEN

FINLAND

NORWAY

Oslo

Lake Onega

Lake Ladoga

Helsinki

St. Petersburg

Lake Vanern

Stockholm

ESTONIA

Lake Vattern

Volga River

North Sea

DENMARK

Copenhagen

LATVIA

Moscow

R U S S I A

Baltic Sea

LITHUANIA

RUS.

NETH. Hamburg

NORTH EUROPEAN PLAIN

BELARUS

CENTRAL RUSSIAN UPLAND

Ural River

Amsterdam

Berlin

POLAND

Don River

KAZAKHSTAN

GERMANY

Bonn

Warsaw

EL.

Volgograd

LUX.

Kiev

Rhine River

CZECH REPUBLIC

U K R A I N E

Volga River

Munich

Vienna

SLOVAKIA

Danube River

CARPATHIAN MOUNTAINS

Caspian Sea

SWITZ. LIECH.

AUSTRIA

Budapest

MOLDOVA

ALPS

HUNGARY

Mt. Blanc

SLOVENIA

CAUCASUS MTS.

Milan

CROATIA

ROMANIA

GEORGIA

ITALY

Adriatic Sea

BOSNIA AND HERZ.

YUGOSLAVIA

Black Sea

AZERBAIJAN

SAN MARINO

Danube River

ARMENIA

CORSICA

BULGARIA

AZER.

Rome

APENNINES

MACEDONIA

Istanbul

SARDINIA

ALBANIA

editerranean Sea

GREECE

T U R K E Y

SICILY

Athens

MALTA

NORTH CYPRUS

CRETE

CYPRUS

0   300   600 Mi.

0   300   600 Km.

Scale

30°E

A-550000-792-1-1-1-1

©1990 Rand McNally & Co.

Woodland

The evergreen forests of northern Europe are the only European woodlands that have remained largely unchanged by humans. The climate here has long, cold, snowy winters and short, cool summers.

Nighttime hunters such as the red fox, hedgehog, and tawny owl prey upon a variety of insects, birds, and small rodents. During the day, such animals as rabbits and red deer peacefully munch plants. The pine marten, a member of the weasel family, remains common in these woodlands.

South of the evergreens lie forests of oak, ash, beech, and chestnut trees. The climate here is warmer, and autumn brings bright colors to these trees. The limbs of the trees are alive with birds, especially woodpeckers, jays, warblers, owls, and nightingales. On the shady forest floor, boars and badgers search for food by rooting in the dirt.

Europe has been settled for a long time. Today the continent is densely populated. Many animals of Europe have suffered from the loss of their homes to human development.

Hedgehogs are common in Europe. Their bodies are covered with thick spines. When they curl up into a ball, their spines stick out and protect them from attackers.

By 1919 the European bison, or wisent, no longer lived in the wild. It was raised by people in a protected area of Poland, however, and today it lives in the wild once again.

Unlike the horns of other animals, deer antlers are shed and grown again each year. Only males grow antlers. Shown here is a red deer, which is found in Europe.

Hares and rabbits are similar to each other. Shown here is a European hare. Polecats are closely related to weasels. Wild boars are found all over Europe, North Africa, and Asia. Squirrels are found worldwide; shown here is a red squirrel, common in Europe.

Alpine

In the Alps of Europe, there are many high, jagged peaks separated by deep, U-shaped valleys. Below the peaks, forests of evergreen trees make the air smell of pine. The capercaillie is a bird that is found here and in more northern parts of Europe.

Above the trees are meadows, home to such creatures as the ibex—a type of wild goat—and the marmot—a squirrel-like animal. In spring, the meadows flower with color as wild plants bloom.

Spring also brings more creatures, as animals move higher up the mountains with the warmer weather. In fall, the animals travel back down the slopes as the weather grows colder and snowier. Above the meadows, life becomes more sparse as the landscape becomes barren rock and snow.

The wild animals of Europe compete with humans and domestic animals for living space. People also cause pollution, which harms animals here and around the world.

The ibex is a wild goat that lives in the European highlands. The ibex was saved from extinction, and now many of these animals graze the alpine meadows.

Mountain peaks provide a safe shelter for the lynx. It is extinct in other parts of Europe. The cats are hunted for their fur and because they sometimes kill livestock.

Ground-dwelling birds called capercaillies (left) are sometimes the victims of large birds of prey. The Pyrenees are home to the griffon vulture (above, left), a large, meat-eating bird. The golden eagle (above, right), also a carnivore, is found in most of Europe and Asia. The chamois is a wild goat that can scale steep mountainsides.

Asia

South of the Arctic Circle, northern Asia is a land of evergreen forests. South of the forests lie first a cold grassland and then cold, windswept deserts. At its southwestern edge, Tibet meets the highest mountains in the world: the Himalayas. To the east is Szechwan, a part of China. India is a triangle of land in southern Asia. The warm, wet lands of Southeast Asia lie where Asia breaks into thousands of islands.

Northern Asia
Just south of the northern Asian polar regions lie the forests of Siberia, part of Russia. Below the forests, the cold Asian grasslands reach out from Europe and cross Asia. The cold Asian deserts begin at the Caspian Sea and the Plateau of Iran and continue through Turkmenistan, Uzbekistan, Kazakhstan, China, and Mongolia. They end with the stony Gobi Desert.

The Himalayas, Tibet, and Szechwan
The Himalayas curve through northern Pakistan and India, almost all of Nepal and Bhutan, and southwestern China. The Plateau of Tibet is part of China. These are places with towering mountain spires and barren, windswept landscapes. In the Chinese region of Szechwan, the high mountains descend into gentle slopes.

India
Millions of years ago, India was not yet part of Asia. It was an island, moving slowly northward in the ancient seas. Finally, it crashed into the mainland, the impact forcing up the huge mountains that are today known as the Himalayas. The deserts of northwestern India contrast with the rest of the country, which is warm and wet.

Southeast Asia
The Southeast Asian nations of Malaysia, Indonesia, and the Philippines are made up of thousands of islands. Some of them are tiny, and some are huge. The islands of Borneo and Sumatra are among the largest in the world. This region is warm year-round.

90°E

SIBERIA

120°E

Amur River

MANCHURIA

Sea of Japan

Tokyo

RUSSIA

Lake Baikal

M O N G O L I A

Shenyang

NORTH KOREA

Sŏul

JAPAN

KHSTAN

SOUTH KOREA

škent

KYRGYZSTAN

TIEN

S H A N

GOBI (DESERT)

Beijing

Yellow Sea

TAJIKISTAN

TARIM BASIN

C H I N A

Huang

River

Nanjing

Shanghai

East China Sea

AN

Xi'an

PLATEAU

OF TIBET

Wuhan

River

Chengdu

SZECHWAN BASIN

Chang

Chongqing

T'aipei

Tropic of Cancer

Pacific Ocean

River

Indus

River

H I M A L A Y A S

Lhasa

River

Brahmaputra

Delhi

NEPAL

Mount Everest

BHUTAN

TAIWAN

Guangzhou

HONG KONG

Ganges

River BANGLADESH

Irrawaddy

Mekong

I N D I A

Calcutta

BURMA

V I E T N A M

Manila

PHILIPPINES

DECCAN

River

South

(PLATEAU)

River

THAILAND

LAOS

China

Bay of Bengal

Bangkok

CAMBODIA

Sea

0   300   600 Mi.

0   300   600 Km.

Scale

ANDAMAN ISLANDS

SRI LANKA

BRUNEI

MALAYSIA

BORNEO

CELEBES

MALAYSIA

Equator

SINGAPORE

I N D O N E S I A

Indian   Ocean

SUMATRA

Jakarta

JAVA

©1990 Rand McNally & Co.

Northern Asia

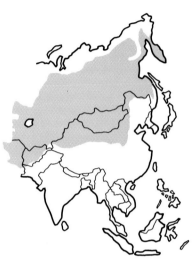

Northern Asia is a wilderness of dark evergreens. The landscape includes bogs, lakes, rivers, and streams. To the south is a grassland that is cut by mighty rivers. It bursts with flowers in spring. The deserts are stony plains under cloudless blue skies.

The Siberian forests are home to much wildlife. The brown bear and the elk are found here. Sables, wolverines, lynxes, and owls also live here. Their prey includes squirrels, chipmunks, and voles.

On both the grassland and the desert, many smaller animals are found. Hamsters burrow below the plains, making systems of tunnels. Polecats, wolves, snakes, and eagles eat the hamsters when they can catch them. A number of birds that nest on the ground live here, too.

The larger animals of north-central Asia include Bactrian camels, wild asses, wild horses, and saigas. The great herds of the animals have disappeared, however, as more and more people have appeared.

The Asian wild ass (above) lives in the driest regions of central Asia. Przewalski's horse (right) is probably extinct in the wild but survives in zoos. It is the last remaining species of true wild horse. This horse is believed to be the ancestor of the domestic horse. There are many types of gerbils.

The two-humped camel has mostly been tamed, but some wild ones are still found in the Gobi Desert. Camels can survive a long time without water.

Wolves live in many places around the world, but in some areas they have been wiped out by humans. Siberia is one of the few places where many wolves are still found.

The Himalayas, Tibet, and Szechwan

Much wildlife lives in the Himalayas and Tibet. Small furry animals–such as pikas, voles, and marmots–scurry to find a meal high up on the mountains. Farther down the slopes are larger animals, such as several members of the goat family. These sure-footed animals are at home on the steep, rocky mountainsides. However, they sometimes fall prey to the skillful hunter of the slopes–the snow leopard.

Szechwan is a land of bamboo forests, where the sky is nearly always cloudy. Here among the bamboo trees live two species of panda. The giant panda may be one of the most well-known animals, but it is, in fact, one of the rarest on earth. Fewer than one thousand giant pandas exist in the wild, and they are rarely seen.

Colorful pheasants come from this part of Asia. Dozens of species of these birds exist. Some of them have been introduced by humans into North America and Europe.

Deforestation, or the clearing of trees, has caused some animals in this part of the world to lose their homes. The large human population of Szechwan is a threat to some types of animals.

The most common prey of the snow leopard is the Siberian ibex, a wild goat. However, the most threatening hunters to ibexes are not leopards–they are humans.

Although the red, or lesser, panda is more common than its giant relative, it is less known. Red pandas are excellent climbers and live in the bamboo forests of western China.

The snow leopard is one of the
most endangered animals in the world.
Yet, these cats are still killed, and their
beautiful fur is used to make coats.

Silk moths make silk. The thick fur of the yak keeps it warm on the snowy
heights of the Plateau of Tibet. The rare giant panda, not discovered by
humans until 1869, lives only in a small region of China. The monkey
known as the Hanuman langur is common in this part of Asia.

India

Indian winters are cool and dry. There are few clouds in the sky. In March, the temperatures begin to rise, and it grows very hot. In June, the season of heavy rains arrives. The air is thick, and it rains every day.

Animals from Africa and northern Asia found their way to India. The hyena and jackal are two such animals. Another animal that lives in both Africa and India is the mongoose. Closely related to mongooses are civets, which live in forests all over southern Asia.

India has the second largest human population of all the nations in the world. As a result, people and animals compete for space. People, who need land for cities, houses, and farms, are winning the battle. Therefore, the homes of many beautiful Indian animals are being destroyed. In regions far away from people, however, rare Indian animals can still be found.

Cobras such as this Indian cobra have hoods at the neck. These poisonous snakes rear up and spread their hoods when they are frightened or excited.

Peafowl may still fly free in the thickest Indian forests. Water buffalo are found in the wild only in regions that are far from people. Tigers are the largest of all cats. Only a few thousand tigers survive in India. The Asian elephant is smaller, with far smaller ears, than the African elephant.

The gharial is a type of crocodile found in the rivers of India. It has a narrow jaw and snout. It is considered sacred by some Indians.

Southeast Asia

Far away from the crowded cities of Southeast Asia lie places that are hard for people to reach. Mountains with sharp ridges and deep gorges make traveling difficult. Hot, wet forests with dense, tangled plants make it even harder. Along the many miles of coast, mangrove trees grow, their roots forming tangles in the swampy waters.

The Southeast Asian rain forests are home to a great variety of wildlife. In the treetops, reptiles, frogs, and squirrels have developed webbed limbs that catch the air and let them glide from tree to tree. The colugo is a gliding animal that is not clearly related to any other animal.

Several types of monkeys are also suited to life in the trees. One type of monkey has a huge nose and lives in the rain forests of Borneo. Bats flit about in the night forest.

The nations of Southeast Asia are among the world's most densely populated. As a result, the tropical forests here are quickly disappearing. Wild animals who live in the forests are becoming rarer.

The orang-utan is a large red ape that lives in trees. Found only in the forests of Sumatra and Borneo, orang-utans are endangered, a result of hunting and habitat loss.

Mudskippers are fish that can breathe air. They spend about as much time out of water as in it. Mudskippers live along warm, muddy shores of mangrove swamps.

The huge eyes of the tarsier help it to find prey in the dark. Tarsiers are related to apes and monkeys and live only in Southeast Asia.

The clouded leopard is a skilled climber that can run down trees head first. Flying foxes are not foxes at all, but bats. Found in South America as well as Southeast Asia, tapirs may look like pigs or elephants but are in fact related to horses and rhinoceroses.

Africa and the Middle East

Much of northern and some of southern Africa is dry, rocky desert. South of the Sahara, curving around to the east, and reaching into the south are grasslands known as savanna. The equator runs through the middle of Africa. In western Africa, the lands along the equator and to the northwest of the equator receive much rainfall. This is where the African rain forests lie. Along the equator in East Africa, there are mountains.

Savanna

Between the African deserts and rain forests are huge regions of grassland called savanna. The savanna heads from Mali, through Nigeria, and into the Sudan. The grasslands curve through East Africa, and then to the south into Tanzania, then on to Zaire and Angola. In the dry season, July to October, the savanna is an ocean of browns. In the rainy season, December to May, the savanna becomes a sea of greens.

Rain Forest

Most of the rain forests of Africa are found in and around the Congo Basin, near the Congo and Ubangi rivers. This area lies on the equator. Most of it is in northern Zaire. It extends into the Central African Republic, the Congo, and Gabon. The forests are also along the coasts of Nigeria and Ghana.

Desert

The world's largest band of desert begins in western Africa at the Atlantic coasts of Mauritania and Western Sahara. It extends across the Sahara of North Africa all the way to Egypt. The desert continues east of the Red Sea into Asia. In southern Africa, the Kalahari Desert covers much of Botswana. The Namib Desert lies along the coast of Namibia.

East Africa

East Africa includes parts of several nations. Among them are Ethiopia, Uganda, Rwanda, Burundi, Zaire, Kenya, and Tanzania. Here the mountains are very tall. As a result, the climate, plants, and animals are different from those of the surrounding grasslands. Between the mountains is the Rift Valley. Parts of this valley filled with water and are now beautiful lakes.

Mediterranean Sea

TUNISIA
Tripoli

L I B Y A

E G Y P T

SAHARA

HAGGAR
OUNTAINS

N I G E R

CHAD

Lake Chad

F R I C A

GERIA

CAMEROON

SAO
TOME
AND
RINCIPE

EQUAT.
GUI.

GABON

CONGO

River

Ubangi

CENTRAL
AFRICAN
REPUBLIC

CONGO

BASIN

River

Z A I R E

Kinshasa

Congo

Atlantic

Ocean

A N G O L A

Zambezi

Okavango *River*

NAMIB DESERT

NAMIBIA

KALAHARI
DESERT

Tropic of Capricorn

Z A M B I A

ZIMBABWE

BOTSWANA

Limpopo *River*

Pretoria

SWAZILAND

SOUTH

AFRICA

LESOTHO

Cape Town

SYRIA

LEBANON

ISRAEL

JORDAN

Cairo

Nile River

Lake
Nasser

Al-Khartūm

S U D A N

Nile

Adis Abeba

E T H I O P I A

RIFT VALLEY

ERITREA

DJIBOUTI

Lake
Rudolf

UGANDA

K E N Y A

RUWENZORI
RANGE

RWANDA

BURUNDI

Lake
Victoria

Nairobi

SERENGETI
PLAIN

Mt. Kilimanjaro

Lake
Tanganyika

RIFT VALLEY

T A N Z A N I A

Dar es Salaam

Lake
Nyasa

MOZAMBIQUE

River

Zambezi River

Baghdad

I R A Q

Tehrān

I R A N

M I D D L E   E A S T

KUWAIT

BAHRAIN

QATAR

S A U D I

A R A B I A

UNITED ARAB
EMIRATES

Tropic of Cancer

OMAN

Red Sea

YEMEN

S O M A L I A

Indian Ocean

60° E

Equator

MADAGASCAR

30° E

60° E

A-580000-792-1-1-1-1

Savanna

The grasslands, or savanna, of Africa stretch out as far as the eye can see. The savanna is a sunny flatland that is filled with wildlife. Some of the most famous animals in the world are found on the African savanna.

In some areas, the grassland is filled with herds of elephants, giraffes, zebras, antelopes, gazelles, wildebeests, and many other animals. These animals roam the savanna, moving across huge distances to look for food and water.

Lions, cheetahs, and wild dogs stalk their prey on the savanna. These hunters hide in the grasses, waiting for the right moment for the chase.

The animals of the savanna share a common enemy: humans. One threat is poachers who illegally kill animals for their hides, horns, or tusks. Another danger is fences farmers put up to hold their herds. These fences do not let wild animals move freely in their search for food and water.

Giraffes can grow taller than fifteen feet (about five meters), making them the tallest animals on the savanna. Their height allows them to browse the upper branches of trees.

A few years ago, African elephants numbered 1.3 million. Today, there are fewer than half that number because they have been slaughtered for their ivory tusks.

The female lioness does most of the hunting for a group of lions. Zebras are among the lioness's favorite prey. When the lions have finished feeding, hyenas might move in and feed on the leftovers. Finally, vultures swoop down from the skies to finish off the carcass.

Reaching speeds of sixty miles (ninety-six kilometers) per hour during a chase, cheetahs are the world's fastest land animals.

Rain Forest

Mandrills live near the floor of the African rain forest, along with gorillas and chimpanzees. Mandrills are the largest type of monkey.

In the rain forest, the weather is almost always the same. Every day is hot and wet. Every week is hot and wet. And every month is hot and wet. Under the high trees, there is not much sunlight. Vines and leaves hang from the trees, creating a world of heavy shade.

The floor of the African rain forest is home to animals like the okapi. These animals are striped and spotted in ways that help them hide from other animals that might catch them to eat. Such larger animals as elephants, leopards, and gorillas also make their homes here.

In the treetops live parrots and monkeys. Rain forests are home to huge numbers of insects. One that lives here is the driver, or army, ant. These insects march along in wide columns and eat whatever may lie in their path.

Like many other forests, the rain forests of Africa are in danger. Many trees have been lost to logging and farming. The number of people in African countries that contain rain forests has been rising. People cut down the forests to make more room for themselves. This means less room for animals.

This bush baby has long hind legs that help it leap from tree to tree. It sleeps during the day and comes out at night. Its large eyes help it see at night.

Chimpanzees are very smart creatures that live in the African rain forest. The pangolin has scales that help protect it from enemies. The striped okapi is a relative of the giraffe. Leopards live in many regions of Africa, including the rain forest.

Desert

In the Sahara, the temperatures are the highest on earth. The amount of rainfall is the lowest on earth. Food and water are so scant that hardly anything lives here at all.

Desert animals have a never-ending struggle to find water. One animal, the addax, never drinks. It gets all the water it needs from the plants it eats. The sandgrouse is a bird that flies far to find water. When it does, it soaks its feathers to take water back to its family. The camel or dromedary is the most famous animal of the desert. Camels can go for long periods of time without drinking water.

The harsh terrain and climate of the desert make it hard to live there, not just for wildlife but also for humans. For many years, the animals that survived in the African deserts did so without fear of humans. The discovery of oil in the deserts of North Africa and the Middle East has changed that. Today the human search for oil creates danger for the animals and their desert habitat.

Meerkats live in the dry regions of southern Africa. When they stand like this, they can see what is happening around the burrows in which they live.

Monitor lizards and scorpions live in several places, including the Sahara. The sting of some scorpions can be fatal to humans. Although they were once wild animals, all one-humped camels are now tame. The tiny fennec fox roams northern Africa and parts of the Middle East.

The oryx once roamed freely over North Africa. This animal was hunted almost to extinction. Efforts are now being made to save the endangered oryx.

The high deserts of northern Africa are home to the Barbary sheep. These sheep belong to a large family of creatures, with relatives all over the world.

East Africa

The mountains of East Africa rise up from the surrounding grasslands. On the plains below the mountains lies the savanna and its wildlife. Some species, like the elephant and black rhinoceros, travel from the savanna into the mountain forests in search of food. Leopards go quite far up the mountains to look for prey.

Farther up the slopes are animals that live only in these East African mountains. In the shady forests lives the mountain gorilla. Several types of monkeys, birds, and hyraxes appear. Eagles and hawks hunt in the mountain peaks.

The tops of the mountains are also known for bizarre plant life. Its strange plants have earned the Ruwenzori Range the nickname "Mountains of the Moon."

The Rift Valley is a huge gash in the face of the earth. The lakes lying in the East African part of the valley are home to their own species of animals. Many types of fish and birds inhabit the waters. Among them are birds that scoot across the water by walking on lily pads and fish that carry their eggs in their mouths.

Only a few hundred mountain gorillas survive. Humans hurt gorillas by hunting them, by capturing them for zoos, and by cutting down the forests in which they live.

Hyraxes are related to elephants and aardvarks. Several varieties of hyraxes are found in Africa. Tree hyraxes are found in the mountain forests of East Africa.

Rhinoceroses are often seen with birds called oxpeckers. Insects living on the rhinos are food for the oxpeckers, and oxpeckers rid the rhinos of these pests.

Crocodiles, hippopotamuses, and flamingos are found near African waters. Like the crocodile, the hippo spends hot African days wallowing in water or mud. The crocodile is sometimes poached, or killed illegally, for its skin. Many flamingos are found in East African lakes.

Oceania

In the south and central Pacific Ocean lie thousands of islands. Australia is an island, but it is so big, it is considered a continent. Most of Australia is very dry, or arid. It receives very little rainfall. Off Australia's southeast coast is the island of Tasmania. Farther away, across the Tasman Sea, is New Zealand.

Arid Australia

Except for Antarctica, Australia is the driest continent. More than two-thirds of Australia is desert or almost desert. Away from the coasts, in the middle of Australia, is a large desert region that Australians call the Outback. Two of the major deserts here are the Great Sandy Desert and the Great Victoria Desert. Like other desert regions, seasons have little meaning here. The sun almost always shines, and the days are always hot. Arid Australia does have plant life. Outside of the deserts, the Outback of Australia is scrubby grassland.

Southeastern Australia, Tasmania, and New Zealand

In the southeastern corner of Australia, rainfall is plentiful. There are four distinct seasons. Across the Bass Strait lies Tasmania, which has a cooler and wetter climate than southeastern Australia.

Tasmania is covered with mountains and hills, with small valleys between them. To the east are two islands called North Island and South Island. Together with several smaller islands, they form the boot-shaped nation of New Zealand. Here green slopes of snow-capped mountains plunge nearly into the sea.

Equator

150° W

Arafura Sea

Torres Strait

PAPUA
NEW
GUINEA

NEW GUINEA

Port
Moresby

SOLOMON
ISLANDS

Gulf of
Carpentaria

CAPE
YORK
PENINSULA

GREAT BARRIER REEF

VANUATU

NEW HEBRIDES

Coral Sea

NEW
CALEDONIA

FIJI

A L I A

GREAT DIVIDING RANGE

Lake
Eyre

Tropic of Capricorn

Brisbane

Darling River

Pacific Ocean

Murray River

Sydney

Adelaide

Canberra

Melbourne

Bass Strait

Tasman Sea

TASMANIA

NEW

NORTH
ISLAND

Hobart

ZEALAND

Wellington

SOUTH ISLAND

180°

0   300   600 Mi.

0   300   600 Km.

Scale

Arid Australia

Central Australia is a land of deserts. Here lie sandy deserts and rocky deserts, mountainous deserts and flat clay deserts. Red rock is all around. Ayers Rock, near Alice Springs, is a huge and ancient piece of red sandstone that rises up from the flat, dry land.

The grasslands here have many unusual wild animals. Kangaroos are one type of animal that lives only in this part of the world. Baby kangaroos grow up in their mother's pouch. Wombats and bandicoots also have pouches for their babies, and they are found here as well.

A number of Australian animals are in danger of becoming extinct. Wombats and bandicoots must compete with animals that people have brought here for the sparse food. Several types of wallabies, small members of the kangaroo family, have become extinct, mainly because of overhunting.

This hairy-nosed wombat is closely related to the koala. Unlike koalas, however, wombats live on the ground, in burrows or warrens.

When scared, the frilled lizard opens wide its mouth, extends a cape of skin around its neck, and sways back and forth. The lizard also lets out a low hiss.

Emus are Australia's largest birds. Their wings are small, and they do not fly. Many of them have been killed because they compete for food with animals that people own.

Wild dogs called dingoes roam much of Australia. Bandicoots are found all over Australia. All members of the cockatoo family of birds have crests. The smallest member is the cockatiel, shown here. Above the cockatiel is a parakeet of central and southern Australia called the budgerigar.

Southeastern Australia, Tasmania, and New Zealand

On the coast of southeastern Australia are forests of uncommon trees that first grew here and nowhere else. Some types are like bushes, while others grow up to three hundred feet (ninety meters) high. And, some of these trees are the food of the koala, which is found only in these forests.

On Tasmania live the platypus and the wombat, along with gliders and wallabies. Here also are three hunters: the Tasmanian wolf, the Tasmanian devil, and the tiger cat. The Tasmanian wolf is not a wolf at all, but a doglike animal that might be extinct.

New Zealand is far from other land, and few land animals have come here from other places. The tuatara lives in New Zealand and nowhere else. It is part of an ancient family of reptiles that once included some dinosaurs.

Some types of birds that do not fly live on New Zealand. The rare kakapo is a ground-dwelling member of the parrot family. The kiwi is another flightless bird. These birds are threatened today, however. The many dogs and cats that people have brought to New Zealand kill these birds that cannot fly away.

Tasmanian devils can kill larger animals such as sheep. Once found in other places, too, the Tasmanian devil is now found only on Tasmania.

Tuataras live on islands off New Zealand. They are rare animals and are the only remaining species of an otherwise extinct family of reptiles.

Lorikeets are members of the parrot family. Rainbow lorikeets are threatened by people who destroy their habitat and who catch them to sell as pets.

Platypuses are unusual animals that lay eggs. Koalas, which are not bears, live in the forests of Australia. Unfortunately, the forests are being cut down. Many species of kangaroos are found in Australia. Shown here is one of the biggest species, the gray kangaroo.

North America

The western part of North America has many mountains. Chief among the many ranges here are the Rocky Mountains. Farther east lie forested areas and, in the southeastern United States, huge swamps. To the south is the narrow strip of land that connects North and South America. It is called Central America. Central America has a climate that is always warm. So do the islands in the Caribbean Sea.

Western Mountains

Beginning in Alaska, a huge band of mountains runs southward through western Canada and the western United States. Many of these mountains are younger than eastern ranges such as the Appalachians. They have not been exposed to the wind and weather as long. As a result, they are rougher and more rugged than the more eroded ranges to the east.

Great Plains

The middle of North America was once covered by a huge inland sea. When the waters dried up, the flat sea bottom became dry land, and the Great Plains took shape. Today, the Great Plains run from the edge of the forests in the east to the Rocky Mountains in the west, and from the Saskatchewan River in the north southward to the Gulf of Mexico. The plains are a flat or gently rolling land, with very few trees, and they stretch out in every direction for miles and miles. The sky seems huge here, and it frequently flashes and crashes with violent thunderstorms.

Eastern Forest and Swamps

Reaching down into the Great Lakes area and the states of the Northeast are the pine forests of northeastern North America. Farther south, they give way to forests of oak, maple, and elm. These extend from the Great Lakes across the Appalachians to the southern coastal plains. Lowland forests and swamps exist in the southeastern United States. Most well-known among the swamplands is the Everglades of Florida.

Bering Sea

ALEUTIAN ISLANDS

Beaufort Sea

BROOKS RANGE

Yukon

Mount McKinley

ALASKA RANGE

Anchorage

MACKENZIE MOUNTAINS

Mackenzie River

Gulf of Alaska

Pacific Ocean

R O C K Y

COAST MOUNTAINS

Vancouver

Seattle

CASCADE RANGE

Columbia River

COAST RANGES

SIERRA NEVADA

Great Salt Lake

GREAT BASIN

San Francisco

Los Angeles

BAJA CALIFORNIA

180°

150°W

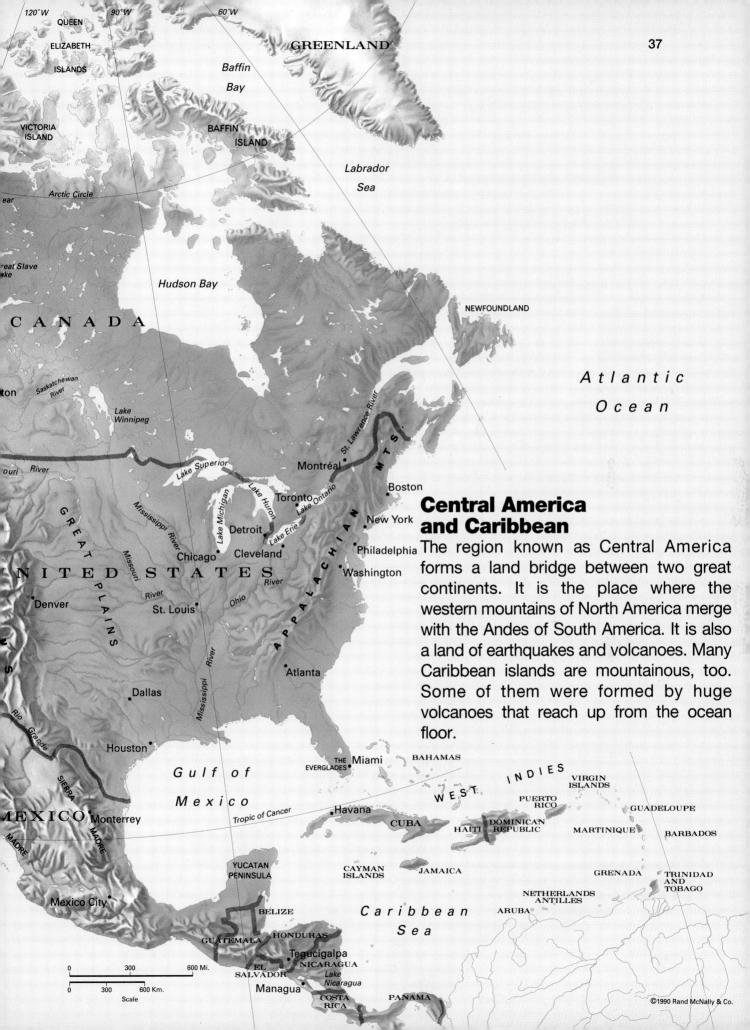

120° W
90° W
60° W

QUEEN
ELIZABETH
ISLANDS

GREENLAND

Baffin Bay

VICTORIA
ISLAND

BAFFIN
ISLAND

Labrador Sea

Arctic Circle

ear

reat Slave
ake

Hudson Bay

C A N A D A

NEWFOUNDLAND

Atlantic Ocean

Saskatchewan
River

ton

Lake Winnipeg

ouri River

Lake Superior

St. Lawrence River

Montréal

A P P A L A C H I A N   M T S.

Boston

G
R
E
A
T

Mississippi River

Lake Michigan

Lake Huron

Toronto

Lake Ontario

New York

Detroit

Lake Erie

N I T E D   S T A T E S

Missouri
River

Chicago

Cleveland

Philadelphia

P
L
A
I
N
S

Denver

St. Louis

Ohio River

Washington

Central America and Caribbean

The region known as Central America forms a land bridge between two great continents. It is the place where the western mountains of North America merge with the Andes of South America. It is also a land of earthquakes and volcanoes. Many Caribbean islands are mountainous, too. Some of them were formed by huge volcanoes that reach up from the ocean floor.

Mississippi River

Atlanta

Dallas

Rio Grande

SIERRA

Houston

Gulf of Mexico

THE
EVERGLADES

Miami

BAHAMAS

W E S T   I N D I E S

VIRGIN
ISLANDS

MEXICO

Monterrey

Tropic of Cancer

Havana

PUERTO
RICO

GUADELOUPE

MADRE

CUBA

HAITI

DOMINICAN
REPUBLIC

MARTINIQUE

BARBADOS

Mexico City

YUCATAN
PENINSULA

CAYMAN
ISLANDS

JAMAICA

GRENADA

TRINIDAD
AND
TOBAGO

NETHERLANDS
ANTILLES

Caribbean Sea

ARUBA

BELIZE

GUATEMALA

HONDURAS

Tegucigalpa

EL
SALVADOR

NICARAGUA

Lake
Nicaragua

Managua

COSTA
RICA

PANAMA

0   300   600 Mi.

0   300   600 Km.

Scale

Western Mountains

The Coast Ranges rise from the rocky Pacific coast. The slopes of these mountains are covered with fir and spruce trees. Ferns grow in the shadows. The Cascades are snow-covered. The mighty Rockies tower thousands of feet, thrusting jagged peaks and ridges high into the cold, thin air. This is the home of some of North America's most famous wildlife.

In the northern mountains lives the grizzly bear. This huge beast loves to feed on the salmon it catches in icy, clear northern streams. Some streams may be dammed, not by humans, but by beavers. Beavers cut down trees for their dams with their big, sharp teeth.

The lynx and the puma are the large cats of the mountains. Among their prey are bighorn sheep, mule deer, and mountain goats. Smaller animals include hoary marmots, minks, porcupines, squirrels, chipmunks, and opossums.

Many protected areas in the western mountains provide the animals with lots of wilderness. Yet, the people of the United States and Canada create demands for land and resources. These demands threaten wilderness areas and wild animals.

Porcupines inhabit forested regions in much of the continent. They rely on their quills and on their keen senses of hearing and smell to protect them.

The national bird of the United States is the bald eagle. These are very large birds that prey on small animals. Pollution and hunting have both harmed the bald eagle.

Mountain goats are found mainly on peaks of the Northwest. These animals prefer living on steep cliffs in places where there is plenty of snow.

Cougars are also called pumas, mountain lions, or panthers. Grizzly, or brown, bears were once more common, but they have been harmed by hunting and loss of habitat. The elk loses and regrows its antlers every year. The horns of the American bighorn sheep (above, right) are permanent.

Great Plains

The Great Plains are sometimes gently rolling and sometimes flat as a table. Except where crops are grown, they are always grassy and always stretching out in every direction.

On the western edge, less rain falls, and the grasses are short and scrubby. Heading east, more rain falls. At the eastern edge, much rain falls. Here the swaying grasses can grow taller than people.

Many of the large animals of the Great Plains have disappeared as more people have appeared. But not the coyote. Coyotes prey on prairie dogs, mice, jackrabbits, and sometimes on pets and livestock. Birds of the Great Plains include prairie falcons and prairie chickens.

The wild grasslands of the Great Plains have been turned into what may be the world's best farming region. As the prairie is turned to farmland, the animals are forced from their homes. Many of them have been hunted to near extinction.

Probably named for its short tail, the bobcat is found in several places—including the plains between southern Canada and northern Mexico.

Coyotes are a type of wild dog. In 1850, fifty million pronghorns roamed the prairie. By 1920, hunters had reduced that number to about thirteen thousand. The American bison was slaughtered, too. Both nearly became extinct, but efforts were made to save them.

Rattlesnakes, named for the rattles on their tails, are poisonous snakes that squirt venom through their fangs into their victims.

The black-tailed prairie dog lives in burrows on the Great Plains. These burrows are connected, forming prairie-dog towns that may take up many acres.

Eastern Forests and Swamps

In summer, the green trees shade the cool forest floor. Fall brings splashes of color, as the leaves turn yellow, gold, red, and brown, and then fall from the trees. In winter, the thin rays of the sun fall through the bare branches but do little to warm the silent, snowy forest. Spring brings another colorful display as wildflowers bloom. Such are the four seasons in the eastern forests of North America.

At one time, a squirrel hopping through the highest tree branches could go from Pennsylvania to Alabama without touching the ground. Today, much of the eastern forest has been cut down. Some animals, such as wolves and mountain lions, have disappeared. Foxes, weasels, and skunks are now the main hunters. They feed on such smaller animals as squirrels, chipmunks, and mice.

As the squirrel headed southeast, it would find the land getting lower and swamps and marshes more common. The types of trees would change, too. At the tip of Florida, it would find itself in the mangroves and cypresses of the Everglades. These swamps are being drained to make farmland. Also, they are polluted by people.

White-tailed deer are found in eastern forests. As male deer get older, their antlers grow more branches, or points. These deer are born with white spots, which fade as they mature.

Bullfrogs live in the ponds and marshes of eastern North America. They wait in the water for insects to fly by. Then the frogs leap to catch their meal.

In the forests of North America lives the black bear. Black bears are smaller than brown bears. Like most bears, black bears eat almost anything they can find.

Cottontail rabbits and raccoons thrive in eastern North America. Alligators and great white herons live in the swamps of southeastern North America. Alligators were hunted for their skins until they were in danger of extinction. Now they are protected, and there are more of them.

Central America and the Caribbean

High in the mountains of Central America are regions where clouds sweep over the rich green plantlife. Meadows are found here as well. Below lie forests and swamps.

In the forests, small wild cats such as the margay cat and the ocelot prowl in the night. They take such prey as monkeys, opossums, and iguanas.

The forests are far from silent, as they are home to a great number of birds. Some birds spend winters here and fly to North America in the spring. Howler, spider, and woolly monkeys hang from the branches with the aid of their tails, which can wrap and grip.

The islands of the Caribbean are far away from the mainland. Large wild animals have never found their way out to them. Birds are the main form of wildlife here, and many of the islands have their own type of parrot.

Destruction of the parrots' homes and hunting threaten the parrots of the Caribbean. Many of them are endangered. These birds are not the only animals in danger in this region, as deforestation and hunting continue to threaten the wildlife of Central America.

The bright-red plumage of the scarlet ibis becomes more intense as the bird gets older. These birds live in swamps, and their long bills are used to probe the mud for food.

The iguana family consists of many different lizards, including the green iguana shown here. Green iguanas inhabit forests of Central America and the Caribbean.

The most serious threat to margay cats is the fur trade. Thousands of these beautifully spotted cats are killed each year. Margay cats are found throughout Central America.

Little is known about the kinkajou. The quetzal is known for its long, bright green tail feathers. Tapirs are found in Central America as well as Southeast Asia. The long snouts of anteaters help them locate ants and termites. The bony plates of the armadillo protect it from attackers.

South America

The Amazon River cuts across northern South America, forming the largest river system in the world along the way. Along the Amazon River and some coasts of Brazil are the great rain forests of South America. The peaks of the Andes form the world's longest chain of mountains. They run down the entire western side of South America. In the Pacific Ocean, off the west coast of South America, lie the Galápagos Islands.

Rain Forest

The hot, wet lands along the Amazon River form the largest rain forest in the world. The forest covers large chunks of Brazil, Peru, Ecuador, and Colombia. Rain forests are also found along the coast of Brazil, near Rio de Janeiro. Rain forests have many different types of animals. Scientists think that nearly one-quarter of all animal species alive in the world today live in South America.

Andes

The Andes are found in every nation in western South America: Colombia, Ecuador, Peru, Bolivia, Chile, and Argentina. After the Himalayas of Asia, the Andes are the second highest mountain range in the world. They are the world's longest chain of mountains.

Galápagos Islands

About 600 miles (960 kilometers) off the coast of northwestern South America lie the Galápagos. They are part of the nation of the Ecuador. There are thirteen main islands in the group.

Caribbean Sea

60° W

N

Caracas

Lake
Maracaibo

Orinoco River

VENEZUELA

Angel Falls

GUYANA

LLANOS

GUIANA HIGHLANDS

SURINAME

FRENCH GUIANA

Santa Fe
de Bogotá

COLOMBIA

ANDES

GALÁPAGOS
ISLANDS

Quito

ECUADOR

Negro R.

Equator

Belém

Manaus

Amazon River

Tapajós River

Fortaleza

Pacific
Ocean

SELVAS

ANDES

PERU

B R A Z I L

B R A Z I L I A N

H I G H L A N D S

Lima

Lake Titicaca

BOLIVIA

La Paz

M A T O
G R O S S O
P L A T E A U

Brasília

ANDES

ATACAMA DESERT

G R A N   C H A C O

Paraguay R.

PARAGUAY

Asunción

Iguaçu
Falls

Rio de Janeiro

São Paulo

Tropic of Capricorn

Córdoba

Mount
Aconcagua

Santiago

C H I L E

A R G E N T I N A

ANDES

Paraná River

PAMPA

URUGUAY

Atlantic Ocean

Buenos Aires

Rio de la Plata

Montevideo

PATAGONIA

0   300   600 Mi.

0   300   600 Km.

Scale

FALKLAND
ISLANDS

Cape Horn

©1990 Rand McNally & Co.

Rain Forest

Macaws live in the highest branches of the forest. The birds' main enemies are people who catch them to sell as pets. The hyacinth macaw may become extinct for this reason.

The golden lion tamarin monkey is very rare. It is endangered as a result of being captured and sold as a pet. Only about four hundred live in the wild.

In the South American rain forest, the Amazon River runs muddy and red. There is no change of seasons here. It is always rainy and hot. The trees, their leaves, and the vines are tangled and thick. The trees of the rain forest crawl with life from top to bottom, with different animals living at different levels.

Hundreds of species of colorful birds fill the trees. Toucans and parrots are two types of birds that sometimes wrestle each other with their large bills. Spider monkeys and howler monkeys call loudly to one another and swing with their tails wrapped around vines and branches. The largest of all snakes, the anaconda, slithers among the trees and reaches lengths of up to thirty-five feet (about eleven meters).

In the waters of the forest live the fierce flesh-eating piranha fish and the caiman, a relative of the alligator. Electric eels lurk in the depths, shocking their prey with volts of electricity.

Today, the rain forest is in danger. Huge portions of it are being cleared. Many experts fear this is causing extreme damage to the wildlife here and to world ecology.

The boa constrictor kills its prey by wrapping around it and squeezing. Boas are not poisonous, however, and will usually flee when they see humans.

Jaguars resemble leopards but are larger. Some animals of the forest come out only at night. They include huge, hairy tarantulas, blood-sucking vampire bats, and slow-moving sloths. Though some of these animals appear fierce, they are rarely dangerous to humans.

Andes

Traveling up the Andes Mountains, observers find that the landscape and climate change. So do the animals. At the bottom of the mountains are forests. Here such animals as ocelots and coatis are found. At the very peaks, the landscape is rocky and rugged, and the climate is harsh. Here only very tough plants and animals can survive.

Three of the animals of the Andes are related to one another and to the camels of Africa and Asia. Llamas and alpacas are two of these animals. Today, all llamas and alpacas are tame, but they once roamed wild in the mountains. Vicuñas, the smallest and rarest of the three, live only in the high grasslands.

Birds live at the greatest heights of the Andes. Some of these small birds have been nicknamed "miners," because they dig burrows in the ground to protect them from the harsh climate. This is also where the Andean condor lives.

Colorful torrent ducks brave the cold, fast-flowing streams of the high Andes. The Andean condor, a member of the vulture family, is one of the world's largest birds. White markings on the faces of spectacled bears have given them their name. They are the only bears in South America.

A few years ago, vicuñas were endangered. Since becoming protected, their number has increased. Most vicuñas live in Peru.

Humans tamed the sturdy, woolly llama as long as four thousand years ago. Millions of llamas are kept by humans in the Andes, for transportation and for wool.

Galápagos Islands

Rocks, cacti, and strange animals are found on these islands. So far away from any major land region are they that few animals ever reached them. Those that did–mainly reptiles, birds, and sea creatures–became different from animals in other places.

Sometimes, the same animal appears in slightly different forms on several different islands. For example, at least fifteen types of birds called finches live here. Each type has a slightly different bill. On the different islands, the tortoises that live here have slightly different shells.

Many of the unique creatures of the Galápagos are in danger. Many have been hunted too much by humans and by the cats and dogs that humans have brought to the islands.

Crabs of the Galápagos share the shoreline with marine iguanas. These crabs sometimes eat the ticks that live on the iguanas.

This iguana that lives solely in the Galápagos is the only lizard that regularly swims in water. These marine iguanas can be four feet (over one meter) long.

The Galápagos hawk is a superb hunter that sometimes kills animals owned by people. As a result, people have killed many of these birds.

The cormorant shown here is a bird that cannot fly. Notice the small wings of this flightless bird. This iguana is a land iguana and, unlike the marine iguana, it does not swim. The shells of Galápagos tortoises vary from one island to another.

Polar Regions

The map shows labels: 120°E, Lena River, R, 150°E, Sea of Okhotsk, 180°, Bering Sea, ALEUTIAN, ISLANDS, Beaufo Sea, Yukon River, UNITED STATES (ALASKA), Gulf of Alaska, Gre, Mackenzie River, ROCKY MOUNTAINS, 150°W, C, 120°W

Around the North Pole is the region known as the Arctic. The Arctic falls within an imaginary line called the Arctic Circle. It is a region that includes the Arctic Ocean, many islands, the northern parts of Europe, Asia, and North America, and most of Greenland. Antarctica, at the South Pole, is a land mass that is larger than Europe or Australia. Most of the continent of Antarctica falls within the Antarctic Circle, another imaginary line.

The Arctic

North of the Arctic Circle, the sun never sets on the longest days of the year, which occur in June. It does not rise at all on the shortest days of the year, which fall in December. The Arctic is blanketed with ice and snow for much of the year. It is too cold for humans and most animals. Almost all the ice and snow melt, however, when summer comes.

Antarctica

At the South Pole, the shortest days are in June and the longest are in December. Unlike the Arctic, much of Antarctica is always covered with ice and snow. It never melts. Surrounding the South Pole is the loneliest, most bitterly cold region on earth. The temperatures here fall much lower than they ever do at the North Pole. The only humans here are scientists and other people who stay for short periods.

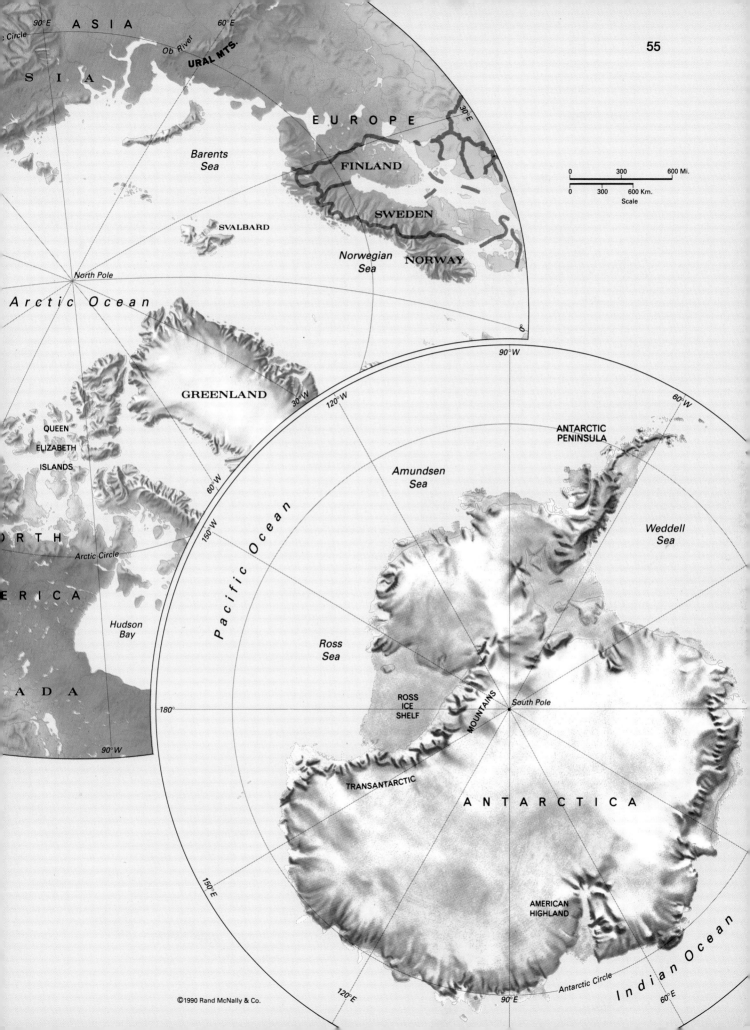

A S I A

90°E

; Circle

60°E

Ob River

URAL MTS.

E U R O P E

30°E

Barents
Sea

FINLAND

SVALBARD

SWEDEN

Norwegian
Sea

NORWAY

North Pole

Arctic Ocean

GREENLAND

30°W

QUEEN

ELIZABETH

ISLANDS

60°W

150°W

Pacific Ocean

90°W

120°W

ANTARCTIC
PENINSULA

Amundsen
Sea

Weddell
Sea

ORTH

Arctic Circle

ERICA

Hudson
Bay

ADA

180°

90°W

Ross
Sea

ROSS
ICE
SHELF

MOUNTAINS

South Pole

TRANSANTARCTIC

A N T A R C T I C A

150°E

AMERICAN
HIGHLAND

120°E

90°E

Antarctic Circle

60°E

Indian Ocean

60°W

300   600 Mi.

300   600 Km.

Scale

©1990 Rand McNally & Co.

The Arctic and Antarctica

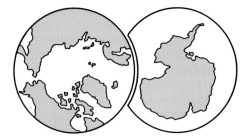

Much life of the Arctic is in the seas, which warm up during summer months. The frozen winter ice cap is almost free of creatures, except for an occasional walrus, seal, or polar bear. In spring the Arctic tundra, or plain, blossoms with life. Here such creatures as musk oxen, reindeer, wolves, and lemmings are found. The coasts are crowded with birds spending the summer here.

The temperatures of most of Antarctica always stay well below freezing. The climate inland from the coasts is so cold that neither humans nor animals are able to withstand it. Only along the seacoasts, where it is warmer, are many animals found. Several species of seals and penguins live on these coasts. Many whales live in the waters off the Antarctic coasts.

People have harmed the polar regions and their animals. Many polar creatures are killed for their thick, warm furs or for such items as oils and tusks. The drilling and transport of oil in the Arctic have resulted in oil leaks and spills that have killed millions of animals.

The polar bear is the largest meat-eating animal that lives on land. Never straying far from water, its main prey is seals. Polar bears live in the areas around the North Pole.

Puffins spend most of their lives on the open
seas and come ashore only to nest. They dig
burrows along the coasts of northern Europe,
Greenland, and North America.

Penguins are a common sight on the lands and
in the waters surrounding the South Pole. One
common type of penguin, the adelie penguin, is
shown here.

The coat of the arctic fox and the feathers of the snowy owl change with the seasons. Musk
oxen, with their shaggy, thick coats, are well suited to life in the Arctic. Caribou and reindeer
were once considered two different animals. Today they are classified as a single species.

Oceans

The oceans of the world are all linked together. They form one huge body of water that covers more than 70 percent of the earth. Land separates this huge body of water into different oceans. Other large bodies of salt water, some called seas or gulfs, are also part of the world ocean. Coral reefs, made up of living coral animals, are found in warm oceans around the world.

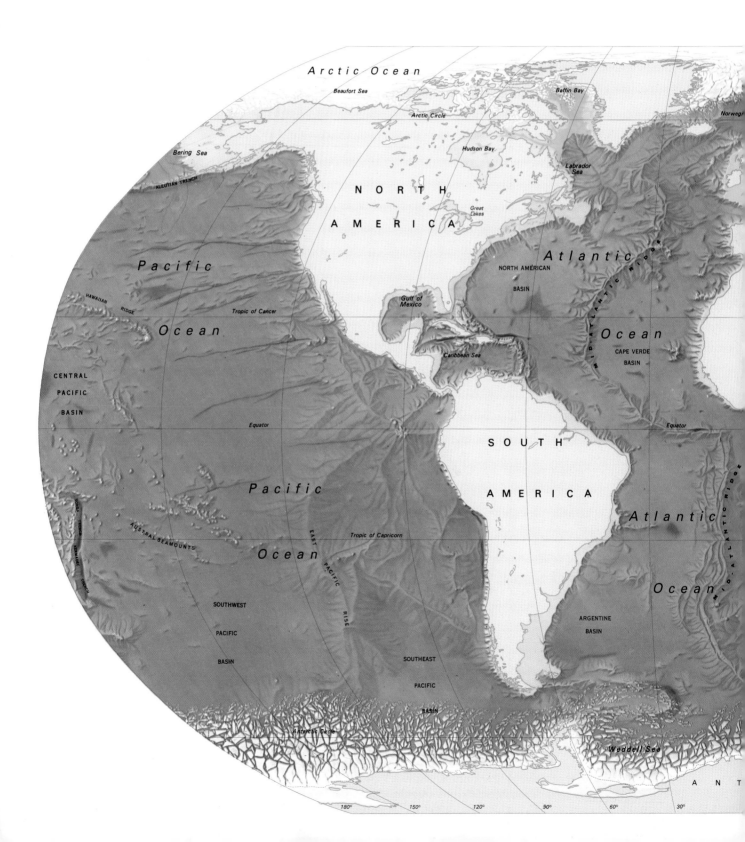

Open Sea

The oceans of the world are the Atlantic, Pacific, Indian, and Arctic. Major seas include the Mediterranean, Arabian, and Caribbean. The Gulf of Mexico is another major body of salt water.

Coral Reef

Coral reefs are found in many warm sea regions around the world. The major reef regions are in the Caribbean Sea and the Indian and Pacific oceans, between the Tropic of Cancer and the Tropic of Capricorn.

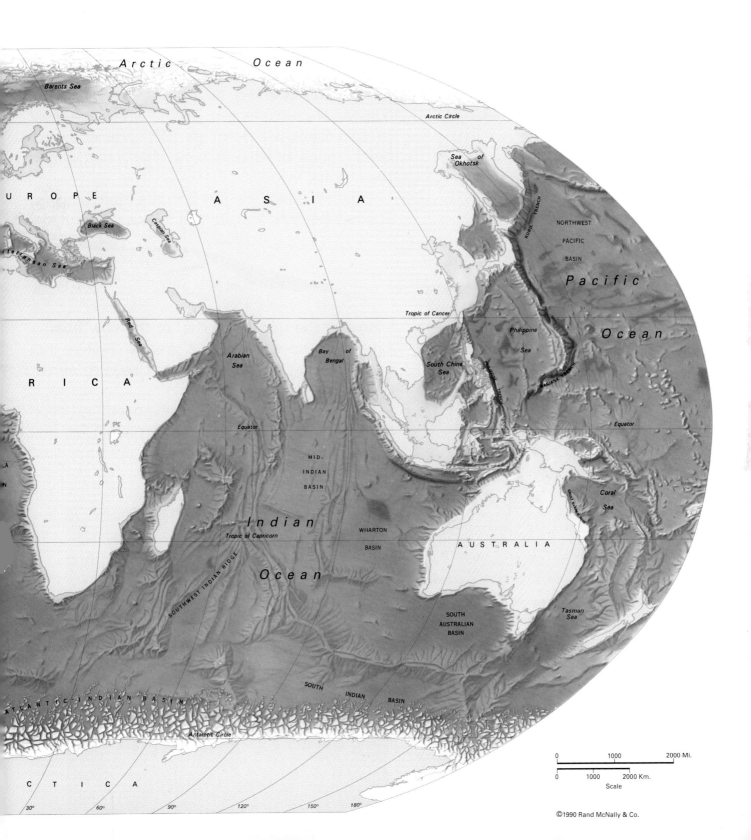

Scale

©1990 Rand McNally & Co.

Open Sea

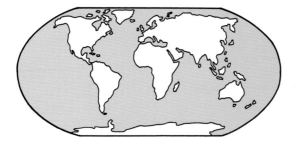

In the world's oceans, animal life depends on plant life, just as it does on land. Plants are eaten by some animals. These animals are eaten by other, perhaps larger, animals, which are eaten by even larger animals, and so on. The smallest plants and animals of the deep are called plankton. At the top of the food chain are such large meat-eaters as sharks.

Near the ocean surface, where the water is lighted and warmed by the sun, the greatest number of creatures live. This is where the most familiar fishes live. Herrings and sardines live in great groups, or schools, while sharks and whales swim alone.

Farther down, the fish become more unusual. The hatchet fish, for example, glows in the murky

waters of the middle depths. At the very bottom lurks the deep-sea angler, a strange creature that has a glowing spiny ray, which it uses to attract prey.

For many years, humans have used the ocean as a dumping ground. Now, some people fear that the effects of all the pollution are only just beginning to show.

Most rays, such as these eagle rays, live in warm waters. Eagle rays have poisonous spines, which trail behind them. Rays can be twenty feet (six meters) across.

The eight-armed octopus is found in almost all oceans. Octopuses are considered to be fairly intelligent. Some species may span thirty feet (nine meters).

The albatross spends most of its life out on the open sea. Whales and dolphins are warm-blooded, intelligent creatures. Both have suffered greatly at the hands of hunters and fishermen. So has the leatherback, the largest of sea turtles. Sharks appear worldwide.

With more than eighty species, gulls are found all over the world. Like many types of birds, most gulls fly to different areas during different seasons.

Coral Reef

Coral reefs can look like patterned carpets on the ocean floor. The living corals rise up in complex shapes. In them live a large variety and number of brilliantly colored sea creatures.

Coral may form less than half of the reef. Various algae make up an important part of the reef. Starfish and sea urchins feed on coral and algae and are often found in the reef habitat.

Giant clams, shrimp, and crabs live here as well. But the most spectacular residents of the reef are the fish that flit among the corals, creating an ever-changing rainbow of color.

Environmentalists are concerned about coral reefs. Pollution in the world's oceans can wipe out reefs. Coral reefs are in danger partly because they are so often found close to shore, where there is more pollution.

Corals are mined for building materials, jewelry, and other goods. As a result, some reefs have been destroyed.

Corals are living animals that form part of the reef. Several forms of sea anemones live here, too, and some attach themselves to corals. Colorful angelfish and triggerfish are commonly found near reefs. The triggerfish is the largest fish shown here. Hiding among the corals are eels.

Perhaps more feared than sharks, barracudas can grow up to ten feet (three meters) long. They can be dangerous to humans.

The zebra-striped lionfish is common in coral reefs of the Indian and Pacific oceans. The spines of the lionfish are poisonous and protect the fish from enemies.

Index to Major Places on the Maps